Our Canadian Flag

Written by

Maxine Trottier

Illustrated by

Brian Deines

Scholastic Canada Ltd.

Toronto New York London Auckland Sydney
Mexico City New Delhi Hong Kong Buenos Aires

Long ago, no flag flew over our country. Maple leaves fluttered like pennants of green in summer. In autumn, they waved their banners of orange, yellow and scarlet. There were many other trees, but it was the maple that people took into their hearts. It was the maple leaf that became Canada's flag.

Native peoples were using maple trees as a source for food long before Europeans arrived in Canada. Slashing the trees and collecting the sap was a yearly event in the maple camps. The Algonquins called maple syrup *sinzibuckwud*, which means "drawn from wood." As early as 1671, the Jesuit missionary priests wrote about the Native use of maple water. The French *habitants*, unable to afford expensive white sugar, quickly learned to make maple sugar of their own.

It is a simple thing, this flag — two bars of bright red, with a red maple leaf against white. But Canada's flag is more than a piece of cloth. It is the story of our country and its people.

"I believe most sincerely that it is now time for Canadians to unfurl a flag that is truly distinctive and truly national in character; as Canadian as the maple leaf which should be its dominant design; a flag easily identifiable as Canada's; a flag which cannot be mistaken for the emblem of any other country; a flag of the future which honours also the past; Canada's own and only Canada's."
— *Prime Minister Lester B. Pearson, speech to the Royal Canadian Legion in Winnipeg, May 17, 1964*

You can see our flag everywhere. It is part of our lives. The Maple Leaf hangs gracefully in busy classrooms, and flies above noisy playgrounds where children laugh and run.

Canada has known many flags. In 1497, John Cabot claimed Newfoundland for England. When Jacques Cartier arrived in Canada in 1534, the Royal Arms of France came with him. After the Seven Years War ended in 1763, Britain's Royal Union Flag became Canada's flag, and the Union Jack waved over the Loyalists in the War of 1812. From as early as 1870, a version of the Red Ensign was being flown in this country. Canadians fought under the Union Jack in WWI; they began WWII serving under it, but by 1944 were hoisting the Canadian Red Ensign. After both wars, there was strong feeling that Canada should have its own flag.

It stands watch over the places where we work, and the places where we pray.

In 1964, Prime Minister Pearson knew the time had come. He had a preference for a flag design, but could not get others to agree. That fall, he organized a flag committee of 15 members of Parliament. Thousands of Canadians submitted ideas. In the end, a letter that committee member John Matheson received from Dr. George Stanley, a Royal Military College professor, proved to be persuasive: "The single leaf has the virtue of simplicity; it emphasizes the distinctive Canadian symbol; and suggests the idea of loyalty to a single country." On October 22, the committee chose the single maple leaf. When their decision was presented to the House of Commons, discussion and debate raged for weeks. Finally, at 2:15 a.m. on December 15, the House of Commons voted in favour of the new design.

It marks our days. We raise it in the morning to the sound of "O Canada," and we lower it in the evening as the sun slowly sets.

Many types of maple trees are native to Canada — striped, bigleaf, Manitoba, Douglas, vine and sugar maples, as well as black, red and silver maples. The sugar maple was an important part of life for people here, providing a source of food, heat, and wood with which to build. Its autumn-red leaf was a fine choice for the design of the Canadian flag.

When people come from far away to make Canada their home, the Maple Leaf greets them with its gentle promise of freedom.

The maple leaf emerges over and over again throughout Canada's history. Legend says that it was a popular symbol as early as the 1700s. In 1834, Quebec's St. Jean Baptiste Society chose the maple leaf as its emblem, and Étienne Parent added maple leaves to the masthead of his newspaper, *Le Canadien*, in 1836. Coins issued for the Province of Canada in 1858 had maple leaves running around the edges of the reverse face. When Edward, Prince of Wales, visited Canada in 1860, people lined the streets to see his carriage pass by. Many of them wore maple leaves pinned on their clothing. In 1867, Alexander Muir wrote the song, "The Maple Leaf Forever," to celebrate Confederation.

And when someone is laid to rest, it waves against the sky in a peaceful farewell.

Long ago, no flags marked the territories of the Native peoples. Then the first Europeans arrived and, with the flags of their countries, laid claim to the land. Over hundreds of years, Canada's people came to include newcomers from many nations around the world. Until we had the Maple Leaf, no single flag represented all who live here. The Maple Leaf is a flag for everyone in Canada.

Our flag travels to many places. Into the frozen north, across wide seas and deserts, the Maple Leaf ripples above the people who set out in Canada's name.

Our country's new flag was approved by Queen Elizabeth II on Christmas Eve, 1964. Her official royal proclamation is dated January 28, 1965. On February 15, in a ceremony attended by thousands, the Red Ensign was lowered and folded by members of the Canadian Armed Forces. While "O Canada" played, the Maple Leaf was raised over Parliament Hill in Ottawa for the first time. All across Canada, similar ceremonies took place at noon in each time zone. Thirty years later, Prime Minister Jean Chrétien announced that February 15 would always be National Flag of Canada Day.

It drifts above the earth in outer space, white and red against the silent darkness.

Colonel Chris Hadfield is one of Canada's astronauts. In April 2001, he was part of the crew of the space shuttle *Endeavour* that was delivering a new piece of equipment to the International Space Station. It was Canadarm 2. Colonel Hadfield performed two space walks while helping to install the 17-metre robotic arm; he was the first Canadian to float free in outer space. On the left shoulder of his spacesuit was the Maple Leaf.

We wear our flag on our clothing, our belongings and our faces.

On a fall evening in 1964, Ken Donovan, a government employee, phoned his daughter Joan. She was to meet him at a warehouse in downtown Ottawa and bring her sewing machine. Prime Minister Pearson wanted to see just how the Maple Leaf flag would look, and so samples of some designs had been silkscreened. Joan worked late into the night, stitching and hemming the prototypes. She later said, "I was no professional — I had just sewed some of my clothes before this. My sewing machine wasn't made for such heavy material. But eventually, the flag came together." She had sewn what was to be Canada's flag.

It flutters in the breeze as we cheer for our team.

"**U**nder this Flag may our youth find new inspiration for loyalty to Canada; for a patriotism based not on any mean or narrow nationalism, but on the deep and equal pride that all Canadians will feel for every part of this good land."

— *Prime Minister Lester B. Pearson,*
February 15, 1965

When Canada wins, the Maple Leaf rises proudly above the ice.

Although no one person designed the flag, the 15-person committee is given official credit. The proportions were suggested by George Bist, a WWII veteran. In flag terminology, the distinctive central white square (which is the width of the flag, but half its length) is known as a "Canadian pale" argent. Jacques Saint-Cyr's design for the flag's maple leaf has eleven points; when the flag flutters in the wind, the points seem to multiply.

Our flag streams out during parades, snapping its own beat as the pipes and drums play. Young children hold it in their hands as brave soldiers march by.

"So, at noon today, in this eighth month of our ninety-eighth year as a Confederation, our new flag will fly for the first time in the skies above Canada and in places overseas where Canadians serve."

— *Prime Minister Lester B. Pearson, February 15, 1965*

And on Remembrance Day, when we pause in silence to honour those who have fought and died for our country, the Maple Leaf is there, a red and white guardian of all that is Canadian.

The official colours of Canada — red and white — were proclaimed by King George V in 1921. Dr. Gunter Wyszecki defined these colours for the new flag. It was difficult to find the perfect shade of red; it took months of testing to find one that would not quickly turn to orange in the sun.

Behind that Maple Leaf, there is a story of many people. It stretches from a time when there was no flag until today — and on to tomorrow. Every country needs a flag, a symbol of what is at its very heart. For us it is the Maple Leaf, our Canadian flag.

"The flag is the symbol of the nation's unity, for it, beyond any doubt, represents all the citizens of Canada without distinction of race, language, belief or opinion."
— *Maurice Bourget, Speaker of the Canadian Senate, February 15, 1965*

For my husband William Gordon Doig,
who having spent some time with the Royal Canadian Regiment,
appreciates the glory of a flag.

— M.T.

For the Roo.

— B.D.

The author would like to thank
Kevin Harrington and Rev. D. Ralph Spence, Bishop of Niagara,
for their advice and insight.

Photograph of Maxine Trottier by William Doig

National Library of Canada Cataloguing in Publication
Trottier, Maxine
Our Canadian flag / written by Maxine Trottier ;
illustrations by Brian Deines.
ISBN 0-439-95687-0
1. Flags--Canada--Juvenile literature. I. Deines, Brian II. Title.
CR115.C3T76 2005   j929.9'2'0971
C2004-906840-7

6 5 4 3 2 1   Printed and bound in Canada   05 06 07 08 09